# PERRY PEARS

National Library of Australia Cataloguing-in-Publication entry

Author: Thornton, C., author.

Title: Perry pears / C. Thornton.

ISBN: 9781925110470 (paperback)

Series: Rare and heritage fruit ; Set 1, no.6.

Notes: Includes bibliographical references and index.

Subjects: Pear--Varieties.
Perry.

Dewey Number: 634.13

LEAVES of GOLD ®
PRESS

ABN 67 099 575 078

PO Box 9113, Brighton, 3186, Victoria, Australia
www.leavesofgoldpress.com

RARE AND HERITAGE FRUIT
CULTIVARS #6

# PERRY PEARS

C. Thornton

# - RARE AND HERITAGE FRUIT -

## THE SERIES

————————⟨∘⟩————————

### SET #1

## RARE AND HERITAGE FRUIT

# - CULTIVARS -

1 Apples

2 Cider Apples

3 Crabapples

4 European Pears

5 Nashi Pears

6 Perry Pears

7 Apricots

8 Peaches

9 Nectarines

10 European Plums

11 Japanese Plums

12 Cherries

13 Figs

14 Cactus & Dragon Fruits

15 Oranges

16 Lemons

17 Limes

18 Mandarins & Grapefruit

19 Kumquats,
   Calamondins & Chinottos

20 Rare & Unusual Citrus

21 Nuts

22 Berries & Small Fruits

23 Quinces

24 Guavas & Feijoas

25 Table Grapes

26 Wine Grapes

27 Avocados

28 Rare & Unusual Fruits
   and more...

SET #2

RARE AND HERITAGE FRUIT
# - GROWING -

1 Propagating Fruit Plants (other than grafting)
2 Grafting and Budding Fruit Trees
3 Planting Fruit Trees and Shrubs
4 Care of Fruit Trees (compost, mulch, water etc)
5 Pruning Fruit Trees and Shrubs
6 Training and Espaliering Fruit Trees and Shrubs
7 Harvesting and Storage of Fruit
8 Pests and Diseases of Fruit Trees and Shrubs

SET #3

RARE AND HERITAGE FRUIT
# - PRESERVING -

1 Fruit Preserving (drying, crystallizing, bottling etc.)
2 Cider Making
3 Perry Making ('pear cider')
4 Fruit Wine Making
5 Fruit Spirits and Liqueurs Making
6 Fruit Schnapps Making

www.leavesofgoldpress.com

# ABOUT RARE AND HERITAGE FRUIT[1]

───────○⌀○───────

This book is one of a series written for 'backyard farmers' of the 21st century. The series focuses on rare and heritage fruit in Australia, although it includes much information of interest to fruit enthusiasts in every country.

For the purpose of this series, rare fruits are species neither indigenous to nor commercially cultivated in any given region.

'Heritage' or 'heirloom' fruits such as old-fashioned varieties[2] of apple, quince, fig, plum, peach and pear are increasingly popular due to their diverse flavours, excellent nutritional qualities and other desirable characteristics.

It is much easier for modern supermarkets to offer only a limited range of fruit cultivars (i.e. varieties) to consumers, instead of dozens of different kinds of apples, pears etc. During the 19th and early 20th centuries, however, the diversity was huge. Old

---

1    Note: this introduction is identical in every handbook in the Rare and Heritage Fruit series.

2    The correct term in this case is 'cultivars'; however most people are more familiar with the term 'varieties' and although it is not strictly accurate, we use the terms interchangeably in this series.

nursery catalogues were filled with numerous named varieties of fruits, nuts and berries, few of which are available these days.

What are heritage fruits? 'An heirloom plant, heirloom variety, heritage fruit (Australia), or (especially in the UK) heirloom vegetable is an old cultivar that is "still maintained by gardeners and farmers particularly in isolated or ethnic communities".[3]

'These may have been commonly grown during earlier periods in human history, but are not used in modern large-scale agriculture. Many heirloom vegetables have kept their traits through open pollination, while fruit varieties such as apples have been propagated over the centuries through grafts and cuttings.'[4]

Broadly speaking, heritage fruits are historic cultivars; those which have initially been selected or bred by human beings and given officially recognised names, before being propagated by successive generations of growers, retaining their genetic integrity far beyond the normal life-span of an individual plant; those which are not protected by a private plant-breeders' licence, but instead belong to the public at large. They are the legacy of our ancestors; living heirlooms; part of humanity's horticultural, vintage and culinary heritage.

Fruit enthusiasts around the globe are currently reviving our horticultural legacy by renovating old orchards and identifying rare, historic fruit varieties. The goal is to make a much wider range of fruit trees available again to the home gardener.

This series of handbooks aims to help.

---

3    Whealy, K.: 'Seed Savers Exchange: preserving our genetic heritage'. Transactions of the Illinois State Horticultural Society 123: 80–84. (1990).

4    'Heirloom plant' Wikipedia. Accessed 2013.

## STORIES

Like people, every fruit cultivar has a name and a story. Take the Granny Smith apple, for example - the most successful Australian apple, instantly identifiable with its smooth green skin, exported world-wide, and now cultivated in numerous countries.

This famous cultivar began in the 1860s as a tiny seedling that chanced to spring up in a compost heap. An orchardist by the name of Mrs Maria Ann Smith lived with her ailing husband in Eastwood, New South Wales (now a suburb of Sydney). She was in her late sixties, a hard worker and the mother of many children.

One autumn day, as usual, Maria Smith drove her horse-drawn wagon home from the Sydney markets, where she had been selling the fruit from her orchard. The wagon possibly contained a few wooden crates she had purchased after selling her produce, in which to transport the next load of wares. One or two leftover Tasmanian-grown French Crab apples might still have been lying in the crates, somewhat battered and past their prime. Imagine 'Granny' Smith, her grey hair tucked up inside her bonnet, trudging down to the creek from which the household drew its water and dumping their decaying remains on its banks.

There in that damp spot, sinking into compost-rich soil, the apple pips lay throughout the winter months. Come spring, one of them split open and a tiny white rootlet appeared. It swiftly bored downwards, stood up and threw off its black seed-case, revealing two perfect, green cotyledons.

The leaves quickly multiplied as the seedling grew, Maria spied it next time she walked down to the creek, the hems of her long black skirts rustling through the ferns. She nurtured the infant tree until it grew up and bore fruit. When at last she picked the first green-skinned apple and took a bite, she must have been surprised by the crisp, hard flesh and sharp taste. No doubt she used it to make pies and other desserts for her sick husband and numerous grand-children, thus discovering that this new cultivar was good for both cooking and eating.

She shared the apples with friends and neighbours, allowing them to cut scion-wood from her tree and graft their own cloned versions. Locally, word of the apple's qualities spread.

'Smith died only a couple years after her discovery, but dozens of Granny Smith apple trees lived on in her neighbours' orchards. Her new cultivar did not receive widespread attention until, in 1890, it was exhibited as 'Smith's Seedling' at the Castle Hill Agricultural and Horticultural Show. The following year it won the prize for cooking apples under the name 'Granny Smith's Seedling'.

'The apple became a hit. In 1895 the New South Wales Department of Agriculture officially recognized the cultivar and began growing it at the Government Experimental Station in Bathurst, New South Wales, recommending its properties as a late-picking cooking apple for potential export.

'During the first half of the 20th century the government actively promoted the apple, leading to its widespread acceptance. However, its worldwide fame grew from the fact that it was such a good 'keeper'. Because of its excellent shelf life the Granny Smith could be transported over long distances in cold storage and in most seasons. Granny Smiths were exported in enormous quantities after the First World War, and by 1975 forty percent of Australia's apple crop was Granny Smiths. By this time the apple was being grown extensively elsewhere in the southern hemisphere, as well as in France, Great Britain and the United States.'

'The advent of the Granny Smith Apple is now celebrated annually in Eastwood with the Granny Smith Festival.[5]

Fruit cultivar stories continue to arise in the 21st century. From AAP, February 21, 2010, 'Mudgee Farmer Bruce Davis Creates New Fruit':

'Is it a plum? Is it a peach? It's probably a pleach as it's a morph of the two tasty stone fruits. Whatever it is, it's a love child of the two, accidentally created by a retired NSW farmer.

'Bruce Davis from Mudgee in the state's central west couldn't believe it when he discovered he had grown a cross between a peach and a plum. The fruit looks like a peach from the outside, but resembles a red plum when bitten into. 'The unusual fruit is believed to be the first of its kind ever grown in the state.

'Mr Davis grows peach and blood plum trees alongside each other and believes the peach/plum tree may have grown from compost that contained plum seeds.

'"It's a really interesting piece of fruit and it's very tasty," Mr Davis said.

'A cross between a plum and an apricot, known as a pluot, has been grown in the past, but a peach and a plum is a new combination for NSW, Primary Industries Minister Steve Whan said.

'Industry and Investment NSW Mudgee horticulturist Susan Marte said this was the first time she had heard of anyone accidentally crossing the two fruits.'

---

5    'Granny Smith' Wikipedia. Accessed 2013

## NAMES

The origins of the Mudgee pleach and the Granny Smith apple are two of many intriguing fruit stories, but sometimes the name - or names - of cultivars tells yet another story, an etymological one. Names may be inspired by the place a new cultivar was discovered, by the person who selected or bred it, by the shape, flavour, colour or use of the fruit, by an event that took place around the time of discovery, by somebody's sweetheart, or any number of other factors.

Names, too, may be multiplied.

The Granny Smith apple was discovered after the advent of newspapers. If you forgot what the prize-winning cultivar was called, you could look it up and there it would be, in black and white. This was not the case for many ancient cultivars.

The Granny Smith apple's probable mother, the French Crab, itself boasts twenty-six listed synonyms, probably invented by forgetful apple-growers.

Another instance of numerous synonyms is the French cider apple whose name is Calville Rouge D'Hiver, meaning 'Calville Winter Red'. It arose in the late 1500s, and as its popularity spread across Europe, the first thing that happened was that people translated the name into their own language: 'Teli Piros Kalvil', 'Roter Winter Calville, 'Calvilla Rossa di Pasqua', 'Cerveny Zimni Hranac' etc.

Next, when absent-minded peasants could not remember the name of this excellent red fruit, they gave it another one. Imagine a weather-beaten farmer in some isolated French village scratching his beard and musing, 'It was something to do with "Calville". 'Calville Rouge,' perchance?' Across the valley in another village, a cider-brewer was knitting his (or her) puzzled brow and saying, 'It was something to do with winter, I am thinking, or was it autumn? "Pomme d'Automne"?' Further afield, a third Frenchman shrugged his shoulders and declared, 'Devil take me if I can remember how it is called, but it is big and red like the heart of a bull, so let us name it '"Coeur de Boeuf'."'

Fanciful, perhaps, but this might explain why, on the database of the UK's National Fruit Collection, there are more than a hundred synonyms listed for Calville Rouge D'Hiver.

Words are forever evolving. Even when cultivar names stay the same, the language around them is changing and their original meaning becomes lost in the mists of time.

One example of this is the grape cultivar Cabernet Sauvignon, which is considered a relatively new variety, being the product of a chance 17th century crossing between Cabernet franc and Sauvignon blanc.

'Cabernet franc' can be etymologically traced back to 'French Black Grape' (from the Latin word 'caput' which means 'black vine'). The word 'Sauvignon' is believed to be derived from the French 'sauvage', meaning 'wild' and to refer to the grape being a wild grapevine native to France. 'Blanc,' of course, means 'white'. 'Cabernet Sauvignon' no longer means 'Wild Black Grape' in modern French - that would translate as something like 'Vigne Noir Sauvage'. The ancient cultivar name has now taken on its own meaning and is virtually synonymous with the wine made from it.

It is interesting to compare typical cider apple names with, say, typical peach or perry pear names. French words abound among heritage cider apple cultivars, reflecting their roots in medieval Normandy. To the ears of English-speakers these names may sound rather mysterious and aristocratic, until you translate them: for example, Gros Bois, Jaune de Vitré, Moulin à Vent du Calvados, Noël des Champs, Belle Fille de la Manche, Petite Sorte du Parc Dufour and Groin D'âne translate respectively as Big Wood, Yellow Glass, Windmill of Calvados, Christmas Field, Beautiful Girl of the English Channel, Small Kind of Park of the Oven and Donkey's Groin.

Some names of heritage perry pears give us an insight into the bawdy, rustic humour of the perry-drinking English peasants who originally selected them; Ram's Cods, Startle Cock and Bloody Bastard to mention a few.

Heritage grape cultivars have names that come from all over Europe, particularly France and Italy.

Figs go back even further. Humans were cultivating them around 9400 BC, a thousand years before wheat and rye were domesticated. Their names, in English at least, are often drawn from their colour and their place of origin - Brown Turkey, White Adriatic, Black Genoa, Pink Jerusalem, Green Ischia ...

Peaches, a more 'modern' fruit in terms of their popularity and breeding, often bear invented names with fancy spellings, such as Florda Glo, Earligrande, Harbrite and Dixigem.

### 'IMMORTAL' DNA

Another major difference between stone fruit and fruits such as grapes, figs and apples is their ability to grow 'true' to their parents from seed. Stone fruits are far more homozygous than their ancient cousins the pomes (apples, pears etc.) and the grapes. Growers do graft them, but if you plant their seeds the new tree will bear fruit that's fairly similar to that of the parent tree. This means that the centuries-old grafting traditions, the fierce cherishing, the careful bequeathing and the meticulous labelling that accompany pome fruits, grapes and other heterozygotes are not seen as often in the world of peaches and nectarines. This is why many of their cultivar names seem so different, arising as they do from highly organised commercial breeding programmes of the 20th and 21st centuries.

Unlike the seedlings of say, peaches and nectarines, seedling apples are an example of 'extreme heterozygotes', in that rather than inheriting DNA from their parents to create a new apple with those characteristics, they are instead significantly different from their parents.'[6] (Humans are rather like apples in that way, though not as extreme.)

Returning to our green-skinned Australian apple - 'Because the Granny Smith is a chance (and rare) mutation, its seeds tend to produce trees whose fruit have a much less appealing taste. To preserve the exact genetic code of any plant variety, a stick of the wood has to be 'cloned'. It has to be grafted onto new roots (or planted directly into the ground, but this is uncommon for trees). Thus, all the Granny Smith apple trees grown today are cuttings of cuttings of cuttings from the original Smith tree in Sydney.'[7]

Cloning by grafting means that the heritage trees - and shrubs - which have survived through the years

---

6       Lloyd, John and Mitchinson, John QI: The Complete First Series – QI Factoids (2006).
7       Stirzaker, Richard: Out of the Scientist's Garden: A Story of Water and Food. Collingwood, VIC: CSIRO Pub. (2010).

are genetically identical to their ancestors. Indeed, the heritage plants of today possess exactly the same genetic code as the original trees that arose centuries ago in Asia and Europe. For example, another heritage apple cultivar, 'Court Pendu Plat', is thought to be 1500 years old - the oldest one in existence. Introduced into Europe during Roman times, the living wood from that same tree flourishes to this day, right here in the Great Southern Land.

## RARE AND HERITAGE FRUIT IN AUSTRALIA

Many of the rare and heritage fruits that exist in Australia today are clonally descended from plants brought to our shores by the early European settlers, when few, if any, quarantine laws existed. Good luck rather than good stock monitoring limited the number of plant diseases unintentionally imported during the early days of colonization. Fortunately, by 1879 it was recognised that in order to prevent the introduction of serious pests and diseases, quarantine measures were needed. In 1908, the Commonwealth Quarantine service came into operation and took over local quarantine stations in every Australian state.

However, before 1879, there was no limit to the varieties of fruiting plants that could be imported into this country. Many of those old genetic lines survive to this day but sadly, many others have been lost.

Fortunately, Australia is one of only two countries free of fire blight, a serious and ineradicable disease that wiped out millions of apple, pear, loquat and quince trees in Europe and the USA during the 1900s. This means that when certain heritage cultivars went extinct elsewhere, they remained safe in this country.

Some have now been restored to their region of origin, now grafted onto fire blight-resistant rootstock.

Over the course of the decades since 1879 Australian fruit growers imported (through quarantine) the latest new cultivars bred by overseas agricultural research stations. Year by year, as scientific advances in breeding and genetics were made, the older cultivars fell out of fashion and were swept aside in favour of the new. They, too, became part of our almost forgotten fruit inheritance.

## COMMERCIAL CULTIVARS

Naturally, plant breeders strive to provide the products demanded by the market. Commercial orchardists want to purchase heavy-bearing trees with high disease resistance, whose fruit ripens all at the same time to save on picking costs. Wholesalers want fruit that keeps in storage for a long time without spoiling, and can be shipped without damage. Only firm-fleshed, bruise-resistant fruit will survive modern-day processing. After harvesting, apples, for instance, are tipped into crates, then passed along a conveyor belt through machinery that washes and brushes them clean of insecticides and dirt. This process removes some of the fruit's natural protective coating, so the machines re-apply a commercial grade wax before polishing them to a high shine and pasting a plastic label onto each one. Then the apples are packed into cartons for shipping to markets and stores.

Supermarket shoppers demand visually attractive fruit - large, regular in shape, unblemished and with highly coloured skin. Consumers also choose fruit with extra sugar content and juiciness.

All these characteristics, nonetheless, do not necessarily give rise to the best flavour or nutrition. To pick a tree-ripened fruit from your own back yard and bite into it is to experience the taste of fresh food as our forefathers knew it. Growing and preserving their own food, unconcerned with transportability and long storage times, they aimed for a wide variety of fruits, each of which had a unique and delicious taste.

Rare fruit, heritage and heirloom fruit enthusiasts across the world are reviving our horticultural legacy by renovating old orchards and sourcing 'lost' historic and unusual fruit varieties. Their goal is to encourage community participation and to make a wide range of fruit trees available again to the home gardener.

This series of handbooks aims to help.

## WHY PRESERVE RARE AND HERITAGE FRUITS?

• They provide access to a wider range of unique and delicious flavours.
• We can enjoy the nutritional benefits of fresh, tree-ripened food.
• Biodiversity: The preservation of a wide range of vital genetic material helps to insure against the ravages of pests and diseases in the future.
• They allow a longer harvesting season, with early and late ripening.
• Culture: heritage varieties, with their interesting assortment of names, are living history.

**Collections of heritage fruit trees are precious. Anyone who is the custodian of an old tree should treasure it.**

# CONTENTS

With thanks to Charles Martell and the Gloucester-shire Orchard Trust for permission to include images and pear descriptions from *Pears of Gloucestershire* www.gloucestershireorchardtrust.org.uk

# ABOUT PERRY PEARS

Perry is a traditional alcoholic beverage made by the fermentation of juice from specific pears. Some people (incorrectly) call this beverage 'pear cider'.[1] When perry is made from real perry pears it is a refreshing and delicate drink rivalling high quality champagne.

Perry pears are cultivars selected for characteristics that make high quality perry. As a species, they are thought to be descended from 'wildings', otherwise known as wild hybrids, between the European cultivated pear 'Pyrus communis subspecies communis', (brought to northern Europe by the Romans), and the now-rare wild pear 'Pyrus communis subspecies pyraster'. Fruits of this species are called 'snow pears', 'Pyrus nivalis', from the Latin 'pirus', meaning pear tree, and 'niveum', meaning snowy.

Snow pears, which have silvery leaves, are often planted as ornamental trees because of their beautiful white spring blossom.

Higher in tannin and acid than eating (dessert) or cooking (culinary) pears, perry pears tend to lack the visual appeal of commercial dessert or culinary

---

1    Gallagher, Paul "Pear cider boom angers purists". The Independent (25 November 2012).

pears, being typically small and blemished, and possessing flavours that are unappealing to most people. For perry makers, however, it is what's under the skin that counts. The right balance of sugar, tannin and acidity is required to make top quality perry. Some perry pears have the perfect balance of these characteristics, while most are better blended. The smallness of the fruits is another advantage in the eyes of many perry makers, since most of the complex flavonoids in any fruit are found just beneath the skin, and small fruits have a relatively large surface area.

True perry pears are renowned for their picturesque and colourful names, such as the various Huffcap cultivars (Hendre Huffcap, Red Huffcap, Black Huffcap, Yellow Huffcap, all having an elliptical shape), those named for the effects of their product (Merrylegs, Mumblehead), pears commemorating an individual (Stinking Bishop, named for the man who first grew it), or those named for the place they grew (Hartpury Green, Bosbury Scarlet, Bartestree Squash). Other curious names include Nailer, Mad Cap, Mad Pear, Pig Pear, Early Treacle, Late Treacle, Clipper Dick, Dead Boy, Ironsides, Jug Rumblers, Grandfather Tump and Green Huffcap Of Knight!

Perry pears often have higher levels of sugar than cider apples, including unfermentable sugars such as sorbitol, which can give the finished drink a residual sweetness. They also have a very different tannin content to cider apples, with a predominance of astringent over bitter flavours. The presence of sorbitol can give perry a mild laxative effect, seen in the names of some perry pear cultivars such as the "Lightning Pear", reputed to go straight through 'like lightning'.[2]

---

2     *Grafton, G. 'Perry Making' (1996) Accessed 2013*

'Traditional perry (poiré in French) is bottled champagne-style in Normandy. Perry has been common for centuries in England, particularly in the three counties of Gloucestershire, Herefordshire and Worcestershire, from which the majority of British perry pear cultivars originate. It has also been popular in parts of south Wales and in France, especially Normandy and Anjou.

'In the UK the most commonly used cultivar of perry pear is the Blakeney Red. These trees produce fruit that is not of eating quality, but that produces superior perry.

'The standard reference work on these cultivars of pear was published in 1963 by the Long Ashton Research Station, U.K. Since then, many cultivars have become critically endangered or lost. There were over 100 cultivars, known by over 200 local names, in Gloucestershire alone.

'Perry pear trees can live to a great age, and can be fully productive for 250 years. They also grow to a considerable height and can have very large canopies; the largest recorded; a tree at Holme Lacy in the UK, which still partly survives, covered three quarters of an acre and yielded a crop of 5–7 tons in 1790. Their size often led to them being planted to provide a windbreak for apple orchards. Mature perry pear trees can often produce crops of one tonne, often two. The trees have been known to live up to 400 years.'[3]

Such trees should be cherished, so that they can attain their natural lifespan.

---

3    Oliver, T. *The Three Counties and Welsh Marches Perry Presidium Protocol. Acessed 2013.*

## PERRY PEAR TYPES

'Perry quality depends on the type of pear used. The classification of pears into different categories is more ambiguous than for apples. The best classification is probably that of Pollard and Beech who defined the following categories: Sweet, Medium Sharp, Bittersweet and Bittersharp although they state that the latter category would probably be better named as Astringent-sharp. The citric acid content of perry pears is also of importance, but is not used for classification.'

'SWEET PEARS

These have low acidity; around 0.2% (w/v) (calculated as malic acid), and fairly low tannin content; below 0.15%(w/v).

'MEDIUM SHARP PEARS

These have an acidity of between 0.2% and 0.6% (w/v) and a tannin content of below 0.15% (w/v).

'BITTERSWEET PEARS

These have an acidity of below 0.45% (w/v) and a tannin content of above 0.2% (w/v). Very few pear varieties fall into this category.

'BITTERSHARP (ASTRINGENT-SHARP) PEARS

These have an acidity of greater than 0.45% (w/v) and a tannin content of greater than 0.2% (w/v). These pears have a penetrating flavour which is very striking since the tannin is astringent rather than bitter. This category of pear is unsuitable for eating (due to the harsh flavour) but makes the best perries.'[4]

---

## MAKING PERRY

'Traditional perry making is broadly similar to traditional cider making, in that the fruit is picked, crushed, and pressed to extract the juice, which is then fermented using the wild yeasts that have either been added deliberately are naturally present on the fruit's skin.

Perry production is similar to cider production, however there are some important differences. Perry pears must be crushed as soon as possible after they have been picked, because they do not keep for long. This means that more single variety perries are made, whereas ciders are usually blended from several varieties.

Other differences between perry and cider are that 'pears must be left for a critical period to mature after picking, and the pomace (the solid remains left behind after pressing out the juice, comprising the skins, pulp, seeds, and stems of the fruit) must be left to stand after the fruit is crushed, so as to lose some of the tannins.

'Perry must undergo two different kinds of fermentation, over a long period of time. The first fermentation converts sugars to ethanol and the higher alcohols (fusel alcohols). The second is called 'malolactic fermentation'. This process converts L(-)-malic acid to L(+)-lactic acid and carbon dioxide. It is carried out by lactic acid bacteria which are present in the pear juice. The malolactic fermentation can occur concurrently with the yeast fermentation but more often is delayed until the fully fermented perry reaches 15 C, normally in the late spring or early summer of the year following that in which the perry was made.'[5]

For more detailed information, see our booklet 'Making Perry' in this series.

### A SHORT HISTORY OF PERRY

'The earliest known reference to fermented alcoholic drinks being made from pears is found in the two thousand year old 'Natural History' by Pliny the Elder, but perry making seems to have become well established in the region now known as France following the collapse of the Roman Empire. References to perry making in its later heartland of England do not appear before the Norman Conquest in the 11th-century.'[6]

'In England, perry pears started out as wild pears, growing in the Forest of Dean in the Wye Valley in the west. They began to be selected, propagated, grafted and domesticated by local farmers as early as the 1500s.

'The fruits, otherwise inedible, were pressed for their juice and transformed into an alcoholic beverage, records of which exist in John Gerdard's *The Herball or Genereall History of Plantes* [sic], published in 1597. Traditionally the juice was extracted by crushing the pears in circular stone mill by pulled by a horse or mule. In olden times it was safer to drink a fermented

---

5     *Gloucestershire – Orchards. www.england-in-particular. info Accessed 2013*

6     *Pears and Perry Making in the UK, The Real Cider and Perry Page. Accessed 2013.*

beverage than the local pond or river water, which might be polluted with fatal water-borne diseases. Farm workers were also paid with liquor by a measure of 'gallons per day'.[7]

In the medieval period, France retained its association with pear growing, and the majority of pears consumed in England were in fact imported from France.

'By the sixteenth and seventeenth century, however, perry making had become well established in the west of England, where the climate and soil was especially suitable for pear cultivation. In the three counties of Worcestershire, Gloucestershire and Herefordshire in particular, as well as in Monmouthshire across the Welsh border, it was found that perry pears grew well in conditions where cider apple trees would not. Smaller amounts were also produced in other cider-producing areas such as Somerset.

'Perry may have grown in popularity after the English Civil War, when the large numbers of soldiers billeted in the Three Counties became acquainted with it, and reached a zenith of popularity during the eighteenth century, when intermittent conflicts with France made the importing of wine difficult. Many farms and estates had their own orchards, and many cultivars of pear developed that were unique to particular parishes or villages.'[8]

---

[7]     'Perry pear joins Ark of Taste ' Slow Food Australia (2013)

[8]     Wilson, C. A. Liquid Nourishment: Potable foods and stimulating drinks, Edinburgh University Press, 1993, p.94

## FRENCH OR ENGLISH STYLE PERRY

Whereas perry in England remained an overwhelmingly dry, still drink served from the cask, Normandy perry (poiré) developed a bottle-fermented, sparkling style with a good deal of sweetness.[9]

## DECLINE AND REVIVAL OF TRADITIONAL PERRY

'The production of traditional perry began to decline during the 20th century, in part due to changing farming practices. Perry pears could be difficult and labour-intensive to crop, and orchards took many years to mature.

'Both English perry making, and the orchards that supplied it, suffered a catastrophic decline in the second half of the 20th century as a result of changing tastes and agricultural practices (in South Gloucestershire alone, an estimated 90% of orchards were lost in the last 75 years).

'Many pear orchards were also lost to the devastating disease fire blight in the 1970s and 1980s. As well as the clearing of orchards, the decline of day labouring on farms meant that the manpower to harvest perry pears – as well as its traditional consumers – disappeared.

'It also lost popularity due to makers turning to dessert or general purpose pears in its manufacture rather than perry pears, resulting in a thin and tasteless product.

---

9     *Normandy, World Perry Capital, Welsh Perry and Cider Society, Accessed 8 December 2009*

'In the UK prior to 2007, the small amounts of traditional perry still produced were mainly consumed by people living in farming communities.

'The industry was, however, to a certain degree revived by modern commercial perry making techniques, developed by Francis Showering of the firm Showerings of Shepton Mallet, Somerset, in the creation of their sparkling branded perry 'Babycham'.

'Like commercial pale lager and commercial cider, commercial perry is highly standardised, and today often contains large quantities of cereal adjuncts such as corn syrup or invert sugar. It is also generally of lower strength, and sweeter, than traditional perry, and is artificially carbonated to give a sparkling finish. However, unlike traditional perry it is a consistent product: the nature of perry pears means that it is very difficult to produce traditional perry in commercial quantities. Traditional perry was overwhelmingly a drink made on farms for home consumption, or to sell in small quantities either at the farm gate or to local inns.'[10]

However, perry (often under the misnomer 'pear cider') has in very recent times exploded in popularity. In addition, various organisations have been actively seeking out old perry pear trees and orchards and rediscovering lost cultivars, many of which now exist only as single trees on isolated farms; for example, the Welsh Cider Society recently rediscovered the old Monmouthshire cultivars "Burgundy" and the "Potato Pear" as well as a number of further types unrecorded up to that point.

---

10    *Pears and Perry Making in the UK. The Real Cider and Perry Page. Accessed 2013.*

## USE OF THE TERM 'PEAR CIDER'

'Pear cider' has in recent years been used as an alternative name to perry. The term was first used when Brothers was sold at Glastonbury Festival in 1995: nobody understood what perry was and were told that it was "like cider, but made from pears".[11]

The use of the term "pear cider", instead of perry, has given a new commercial lease of life to a drink that was practically extinct; in two years sales of the drink increased from £3.4 million to £46 million. The brewers Brothers, Gaymers and Bulmers/Magners now all have their own brands of pear cider, and Tesco is also increasing the number of pear ciders that it sells. The brewers see the term "pear cider" as being more understandable to the younger 18–34 demographic.

'The Campaign for Real Ale' defines perry and pear cider as quite different drinks, stating that 'pear cider' as made by the large industrial cider-makers is merely a pear-flavoured drink, or more specifically a cider-style drink, often containing apple juice, flavoured with pear concentrate, whereas true 'perry' should be made by traditional methods from perry pears only.'[12]

## PERRY IN AUSTRALIA

Real perry is also becoming increasingly popular in Australia. Small local manufacturers are beginning to appear such as Gypsy Cider, brewed by 2 Brothers Brewery in Melbourne, Henry's of Harcourt, Victoria,

---

11      *"From perry to pear cider" BBC News Magazine. (28 August 2009)*
12      *Huddleston, Nigel: "Pear Perception". Morning Advertiser (24 April 2008).*

and LOBO Cider in the Adelaide Hills. Perry pear Orchards are also being established in Tasmania.[13]

It is said that perry pears were introduced to the goldfields near Bendigo during the Victorian gold rushes in the early 1860s or before. It provided a low-alcoholic beverage as an alternative to beer, for miners during the Victorian gold rushes. However, only five traditional European Perry pears have been identified as surviving in Australia to the 21st century. These are Moorcroft, Gin, Green Horse, Yellow Huffcap and Red Longdon. In 2013 those five endangered cultivars of Australian perry pear were added to the Slow Food Foundation for Biodiversity's international Ark of Taste.[14]

Australia's perry pears are all 'of the Medium-sharp' type, excepting the rare Red Longdon, which is 'Bitter-sharp'.

Australian commercial perry producers generally use dessert pears, with variable results. Australian Food Standards permit up to 25% of apple juice in perry or 'pear cider'. [15]

'Australia's first national cider-tasting competition was held in the Adelaide Hills in 2007. The overall winner ended up not being an apple cider but a 'pear cider', properly known as perry. It was made in the rural town of Harcourt in Victoria. The Henry family, Michael and his father, Drew, have been making Peary from the brown Beurre Bosc pears (a dessert cultivar)

---

13     ^ "Growing cider apples". NSW Department of Primary Industries. 01 May 2008.
14     'Perry pear joins Ark of Taste' Slow Food Australia (2013)
15     'Perry', Wikipedia. Accessed 2013.

for a number of years, but they have also started collecting traditional pears.

They are gradually grafting their orchard over to older European cultivars and perry pears, which contain more tannins and acids than eating pears.

The Henrys believe they are the only Australian company producing commercial quantities of real perry, although they still make their product in a very traditional way, cold-pressing the pear pulp on a block known as 'the cheese'.

Michael Henry says: "It is a little bit different from apple cider. It's a lot softer, a lot smoother. There are not as many tannins or acids in pears as there are in apples, so apple ciders can tend to be a little bit sharp and have a very tart finish to them. Whereas the perry is a very soft, very smooth, extraordinarily easy drink to drink and has delightful light aromas."[16]

Harcourt Pear Cider is a blend of Buerre Bosc, William and Packham pears which are milled and gently basket pressed. Fermentation is conducted by a Champagne yeast in stainless steel tanks. Post fermentation, the different cider cuvees are blended, filtered and bottled.

### PERRY PEARS IN YOUR OWN BACKYARD

Australian home gardeners who want to grow their own perry pears can now find four of our five precious cultivars by searching for mail-order fruit tree nurseries on the Internet. Gin, Green Horse, Moorcroft and Yellow Huffcap are available online. The fifth cultivar, Red Longdon, is more elusive. Only

---

16      *Adams, Prue. ABC Landline, Cider House Rules,*
*(06/04/2008)*

a small number of these trees exist, under the care of a perry grower in central Victoria. It may be several years before Red Longdon gets wider distribution.

Finally, here's a quote from a classic 18th century poem urging all those who love good fruit-based liquors to care well for their fruit trees!

> 'Would'st thou thy vats with generous juice should froth?
> Respect thy orchats; think not that the trees
> Spontaneous will produce a wholesome draught
> Let art correct thy breed."[17]

---

17     *Philips, John: 'Cyder: A Poem. In Two Books' (1708).*

# RARE AND HERITAGE PERRY PEAR CULTIVARS

## IN AUSTRALIA

# GIN

---

Status: Extant, rare.

Provenance: Mature trees of this heritage cultivar seem to be centred on Highfields, Newent, UK where it may have arisen. Durham asserts that its perry has a juniper flavour, hence 'gin'. A number of perry pear varieties are named, doubtless by their protagonists, after spirits or strong drink, presumably to indicate their quality and strength.

Date: First recorded 1886.

Use: Perry.

Fruit description: after Luckwill and Pollard.

Type: Medium Sharp

Size: 42-58mm. wide, 35-49mm. long.

Shape: Broadly turbinate, approaching oblate.

Skin: Green, usually with an orange flush and sometimes faintly streaked; restricted russet round stem and eye; lenticels small and inconspicuous; scab absent.

Tree: Medium size with narrow angled crotches and slightly spreading limbs with a heavy spur system. Good cropping, sometimes biennial.

## NOTES:

A cultivar with good disease resistance and keeping quality of fruit. Jean Nowell and Kevin Minchew report that this cultivar makes a fragrant perry.

Listed by Hogg and Bull as a 'local' cultivar, it is now considered a high quality vintage pear and at the turn of the millennium is undergoing planting by artisan perry makers.[1]

## REFERENCE:

Hogg, R. and Bull, H.G., *The Apple and Pear as Vintage Fruits*, Jakeman and Carver, Hereford (1886):

Durham, H.E., *Perry Pear Trees and Perry* Woolhope Naturalists' Field Club (1923)

Durham, H.E., *The Beauty and use of the Vintage Pear.* RHS Journal (1924)

Luckwill, L.C. and Pollard, A., *Perry Pears.* University of Bristol, (1963).

Jean Nowell and Kevin Minchew, personal communications (2010). *Pears of Gloucestershire.* The Gloucestershire Orchard Group, UK.

---

1       *Martell, Charles 'Pears of Gloucestershire', the Gloucestershire Orchard Trust. Accessed 2013.*

# GIN

*Original photograph of Pyrus sp. var. Gin fruit by C.Martell*

# GREEN HORSE

—⚬⚬⚬—

Synonyms: Horse Pear, White Horse, White Longland, Rye Court Green Horse, White Longland , White Horse Pear.

Status: Extant, rare.

Provenance: This heritage cultivar was described by Hogg and Bull as White Longland with the synonym White Horse Pear. That was the first known description. Later it was described by Durham as White Horse. It was, found at Dymock and Oxenhall and is possibly the same cultivar as Green Horse and Rye Court Green Horse. Luckwill and Pollard record that it was found throughout north and west Gloucestershire.

Date: First documented 1886.

Use: Perry, but originally culinary as were some other perry pears.

Fruit description: after Luckwill and Pollard.

Type: Medium Sharp

Size: 45-60mm. wide, 36-61mm. long.

Shape: Oblate or may be slightly turbinate.

Skin: Green or yellowish green, may have slight orange flush; russet around stem and more round eye spreading to cheek; lenticels usually white and more conspicuous on russet; scab often present.

Tree: Large with large upright limbs terminating in small branches. A fairly good and regular cropper.

## NOTES:

Attempting to unravel the nomenclature and provenance of this cultivar is a confounding situation to be met with by all perry pear researchers.

Some other old perry pears are named Black Horse and Red Horse.

## REFERENCE:

Hogg, R. and Bull, H.G., *The Apple and Pear as Vintage Fruits*. Jakeman and Carver, Hereford (1886)

Durham, H.E., *Perry Pear Trees and Perry*. Woolhope Naturalists' Field Club (1923)

Durham, H.E., *The Beauty and use of the Vintage Pear*. RHS Journal (1924)

Luckwill, L.C. and Pollard, A., *Perry Pears*. University of Bristol, (1963)

*Pears of Gloucestershire*. The Gloucestershire Orchard Group, UK. (2009)

# Green Horse

*Original photograph of Pyrus sp. var. Green Horse fruit by C.Martell*

# MOORCROFT

———⟨ᴏᴖᴏ⟩———

Synonyms: Choke Pear, Chokers, Malvern Hill Pear, Malvern Hills, Malvern Pear, Stinking Bishop.

Status: Extant, not threatened.

Provenance: Believed to have originated at Moorcroft Farm, Colwall where Hogg and Bull found 'many trees of a considerable age'. Widely planted throughout the main perry producing districts and beyond. Propagated to the NCCPG National Perry Pear Collection, Malvern from H.P.Bulmer & Co's mother tree orchard at Hampton Bishop, Hereford.

Date: First record 1884. Collected for propagation 1990s.

Use: Perry.

Fruit description: after Luckwill and Pollard

Type: Bittersharp (Astringent-Sharp)

Size: 43-57 mm. wide, 44-60 mm. long.

Shape: Turbinate sometimes pyriform.

Skin: Yellow or yellowish green; russet at both ends or only round eye; lenticels numerous, large, whitish and conspicuous; scab may be severe.

Tree: May be very large with few long upright limbs. Rounded head and has the appearance and proportions of a grand oak when growing on good soil. Its bark has distinctive deep vertical striations

## NOTES:

Jean Nowell and Kevin Minchew, personal communications (2010) report that this cultivar makes a fragrant perry.

In the late 1800s Percy Bishop lived at Moorcroft Farm and due to his riotous living earned himself the nickname 'Stinking Bishop'. Hence this name became synonymous with this cultivar.

Andy Shayle of Ashleworth distinguishes between Moorcroft and Malvern Hills Pears, the latter is a later version and has the same characteristic deeply striated bark. Similarly Bill Gooch differentiated between the Moorcroft and Malvern Hills Pears.

Many people have remarked that fine quality Moorcroft perry can be deceptively strong. The symptoms seem to be of feeling quite normal until trying to stand when the legs just won't work, necessitating a journey home by wheelbarrow. The perry got nicknamed 'Wheelbarrow Perry'.

# MOORCROFT

*Original photograph of Pyrus sp. var. Moorcroft fruit by C.Martell*

## REFERENCE:

Hogg, Robert. *The Fruit Manual*. Fifth Edition. Journal of Horticulture Office, London, (1884)

Hogg, R. and Bull, H.G., T*he Apple and Pear as Vintage Fruits*. Jakeman and Carver, Hereford (1886)

Durham, H.E., *Perry Pear Trees and Perry*. Woolhope Naturalists' Field Club (1923)

Durham, H.E., *The Beauty and use of the Vintage Pear*. RHS Journal (1924)

Durham, H.E., MS photo album (1926)

Luckwill, L.C. and Pollard, A., *Perry Pears*. University of Bristol, (1963)

John Bishop, personal communication (2006)

Andy Shayle personal communication (1996)

Bill Gooch, personal communication (2002)

*Pears of Gloucestershire*. The Gloucestershire Orchard Group, UK..

# RED LONGDON

Synonyms: Brockhill (false) Brockle, Cider Pear, Longland, Red Longland, Red Longley, Red Longney.

Status: Extant, very rare.

Provenance: A widespread cultivar first described by T.A.Knight. Propagated from H.P.Bulmer & Co scion orchard, Hampton Bishop, to the NCCPG National Perry Pear Collection, Malvern

Date: A cultivar so old that T.A.Knight considered it 'to be rapidly approaching that period, when it can no longer be cultivated with advantage.' Collected for propagation early 1990s.

Use: Perry.

Fruit description: after Luckwill and Pollard.

Type: Medium Sharp

Size: 51-61 mm. wide, 48-60 mm. long.

Shape: Turbinate or pyriform.

Skin: Green or yellowish green with a strong red or red-orange flush spreading from the eye; russet round the stem and more round the eye spreading to the cheeks; lenticels numerous, large, light coloured and conspicuous, especially on flush; some scab usually present.

Tree: Medium sized, with a few long upright limbs terminating in twiggy growth. Suffers from die-back. A regular and light cropper.

## PRODUCTION IN AUSTRALIA

Only a small number of these trees exist, under the care of a perry grower in central Victoria.

## NOTES:

The cultivar Brockhill was collected for propagation to the National Perry Pear Collection at Malvern from H.P.Bulmer & Co's Broxwood Orchard. This accession was found not to be synonymous with Red Longdon as expected.

Until the 1920s the Longdon pears were termed Longland because according to T.A.Knight 'it probably derived its name from the field in which the original tree grew.' By the 1960s this cultivar was being referred to as the Longdon. Perry pears do grow in the village of Longdon but the question may be asked: Why the change? Luckwill and Pollard do not even give the synonym as Longland for this cultivar.

# Red Longdon

*Original photograph of Pyrus sp. var .Red Longdon fruit by
C.Martell*

## REFERENCE:

Knight, T.A., *Pomona Herefordiensis* (1811)

Durham, H.E., *Perry Pear Trees and Perry.* Woolhope Naturalists' Field Club (1923)

Durham, H.E., *The Beauty and use of the Vintage Pear.* RHS Journal (1924)

Hogg, Robert. *The Fruit Manual.* Fifth Edition. Journal of Horticulture Office, London, (1884)

Hogg, R. and Bull, H.G., *The Apple and Pear as Vintage Fruits*, Jakeman and Carver, Hereford (1886)

Luckwill, L.C. and Pollard, A., *Perry Pears.* University of Bristol, (1963)

*Pears of Gloucestershire.* The Gloucestershire Orchard Group, UK..

# YELLOW HUFFCAP

———————————⟨⟩⟨⟩⟨⟩———————————

Synonyms: Black Huffcap , Brown Huffcap, Chandos Huffcap, Green Huffcap, Huffcap, King's Arms, Uffcap, Uffcup, Yellow Longdon, Yellow Longland(s).

Status: Extant, rare.

Provenance: While Knight asserts that this cultivar must have been known of in the 17th Century, its identity is confused and it is difficult to establish which cultivar of Huffcap an author is referring to until Durham locates and names a particular tree, the Chandos Huffcap which the author remembers at Chandos Farm. Luckwill and Pollard identify this tree as the true Yellow Huffcap, but they concede that the name is often applied locally to many other quite distinct varieties. Propagated to the NCCPG National Perry Pear Collection, Malvern from H.P. Bulmer & Co's mother tree orchard at Hampton Bishop.

Date: 17th Century according to Knight. Described by Knight 1811. First described specifically by Luckwill and Pollard 1963. Propagated ca.1992

Use: Perry.

Fruit description: after Luckwill and Pollard.

Type: Medium Sharp

Size: 35-45 mm. wide, 41-51 mm. long.

Shape: Elliptical.

Skin: Green, yellow or yellowish black, without flush; russet around stem and eye often scaly and spreading on to cheeks; lenticels numerous, usually large, conspicuous brown and corky, merging into russet; scab generally absent.

Tree: Large with several outward curving main limbs ending in dense twiggy growth. A heavy cropper which may be biennial.

### NOTES:

Medium acid, low tannin, makes an excellent quality perry.

The term 'huffcap' has caused some discussion.

Ray Williams writing in 'Perry Pears' asserts that the name 'huffcap' was originally given to a particularly strong ale which implied that the drink was potent enough to lift the cap off one's head. A further possibility is given that the fruit was named after a family of great farming and perry making repute named Huff living in the parish of Dymock.

Tom Oliver, a renowned cider and perry maker recalls his father saying that the pastry covering of a dish would rise up giving a domed crust holding the heat and moisture inside. This domed pastry cover was termed a huffcap. His father had gained this

# YELLOW HUFFCAP

*Original photograph of Pyrus sp. var. Yellow Huffcap fruit by C.Martell.*

information from an old recipe book. Tom still cooks his Christmas ham inside a huffcap.

The sign outside the Mother Huffcap pub in Warwickshire depicts a pint of beer with a good head which is overflowing.

The term 'huffcap' as used above appears to refer to a 'high head'. 'Huff' may derive from the same root as present day German 'hoch' meaning 'high' and 'cap' from 'kopf' meaning 'head' in the same language. Most huffcap pears when viewed from the side have a 'high head' as a result of the elliptical shape they have in common. See also Coppy.

### REFERENCE:

Knight, T.A., *Pomona Herefordiensis* (1811)

Hogg, R. and Bull, H.G., *The Apple and Pear as Vintage Fruits*, Jakeman and Carver, Hereford (1886)

Durham, H.E., Perry *Pear Trees and Perry*. Woolhope Naturalists' Field Club (1923)

Durham, H.E., *The Beauty and use of the Vintage Pear*. RHS Journal (1924)

Luckwill, L.C. and Pollard, A., *Perry Pears*. University of Bristol, (1963)

Ray Williams, personal communication (ca1995)

Tom Oliver, personal communication (2006)

*Pears of Gloucestershire*. The Gloucestershire Orchard Group, UK..

## ROOTSTOCKS

Perry pear scion wood may be grafted onto Quince (Cydonia oblonga), Callery Pear (Pyrus Calleryana), Birchleaf Pear (Pyrus Betulifolia), or European Pear (Pyrus communis). It also does well on its own Snow pear roots (Pyrus nivalis).

# Other Perry Pear Cultivars[1]

## A

American Sickle see SICKLE PEAR

Arlingham see HARLEY GUM

ARLINGHAM SQUASH [Synonym: Green Squash (Evelyn), Old Squash, Old Taynton Squash, Squash Pear.]

Awrel - see OLDFIELD

Aylton Red - see RED PEAR

## B

Bache's White - see WHITE BACHE

Bareland see BARLAND

BARLAND synonym: Bosbury Pear, Bareland, Bearland.

Barn Pear - see BARNET and TURNER'S BARN

---

1    *This catalogue of world-wide perry pear cultivars is as comprehensive was possible it at the time of publication, but should not be considered complete.*

BARNET synonym:       Barn  Pear,  Brown  Thorn
  Pear, Hedgehog Pear.
BARTESTREE SQUASH
Bastard Barland - see WHITE LONGDON
BASTARD LONGDON
Bastard Longdon – see WHITE LONGDON
BASTARD SACK
Bearland - see BARLAND
Beech White - see WHITE BACHE
BEETROOT PEAR – Wick Court Alex synonym:
  (Generically) Blood Pear.
BEETROOT PEAR – Wick Court Ella synonym:
  (Generically) Blood Pear.
BEETROOT PEAR – Wick Court Eric synonym:
  (Generically) Blood Pear.
BETTY PROSSER
Billy Thurston - see THURSTON'S RED
BILLY WILLIAMS
Billy Williams - see NAILER
BIRD PEAR
BLACK HORSE
Black Horse – see RED PEAR
BLACK HUFFCAP synonym: Black Pear
Black Huffcap - see ROCK and YELLOW HUFFCAP
Black Pear - see BLACK HUFFCAP
BLACKSMITH
Blakeney - see BLAKENEY RED
BLAKENEY  RED  synonyms: Blakeney,  Red  Pear,
  Circus  Pear,  Painted  Lady,  Painted  Pear  and
  Brinsop, Red Longtail (Durham: false).
BLOOD PEAR
BLOODY BASTARD
Blunt Red - see RED PEAR
Bosbury Pear see BARLAND

BOSBURY SCARLET
BOY PEAR
BRANDY
BRINARL
BROCKHILL synonym: Red Longdon has the synonym Brockhill and was believed to be covarietal to this variety. It is however quite distinct.
Brockhill - see RED LONGDON (in error)
Brockle - see RED LONGDON
BROWN BESS synonym:Brown Bessie.
Brown Bessie - see BROWN BESS
Brown Huffcap - see ROCK and YELLOW HUFFCAP
Brown Longdon - see GREEN LONGDON
Brown Thorn Pear - see BARNET
BROWN RUSSET synonym: possibly New Meadow
Brown Thorn Pear - see BARNET
BUNCH PEAR
BURFORD
BUTT synonym: Norton Butt
BUTTER PEAR

# C

CANNOCK
Chaceley Green - see HARTPURY GREEN
Chaseley Green - see HARTPURY GREEN
Chandos Huffcap - see YELLOW HUFFCAP
CHAXHILL ROUGH
Choke Pear see MOORCROFT
Chokers see MOORCROFT
CHRISTMAS PEAR
Cider Pear - see RED LONGDON
CIPHROUS PEAR
Circus Pear - see BLAKENEY RED

CLARET
CLIPPER DICK
Cluster Top - see HOLMER
CLUSTERS
Coppice - see COPPY
COPPY synonym: Coppice
COWSLIP PEAR
Cumber - see LUMBER
CYGNET
Dandoe - see WHITE LONGDON

# D

DEAD BOY
DRAKE PEAR
Duckbarn - see DUCKSBARN
Ducksbourne - see DUCKSBARN
DUCKSBARN synonym: Duckbarn, Ducksbourne
Dymock Red - see THURSTON'S RED

# E

EARLY BLET
EARLY BLUNT RED synonym: Blunt Red
EARLY GRIFFIN synonym: Griffin's Early
EARLY HAY PEAR synonym: Hay Pear.
EARLY LONGDON
EARLY TAYNTON SQUASH synonym: Taynton
   Squash, Squash Pear
EARLY TREACLE

# F

FLAKEY BARK
Ford's Green Huffcap - see HILLEND GREEN
FOREST PEAR

# G

Garradine - see WHITE LONGDON
GELBMOSTLER
GENNET – Green
GENNET - Laurel
GENNET – Red
GIN
GOLDEN BALLS
GOLDINGS
GRANDFATHER TUM synonym: Grandfather Tump
GREEN HORSE synonym: Horse Pear, White Horse,
    White Longland, Rye Court Green Horse, White
    Longland , White Horse Pear.
Green Huffcap - see YELLOW HUFFCAP
GREEN HUFFCAP of KNIGHT
GREEN LONGDON synonym: Old Fashioned, Brown
    or Russet Longdon, Longdon, Longland(s).
GREEN OLIVE
GREEN ROLLER
Green Squash - see ARLINGHAM SQUASH
Gregg Pear – see GREGG'S PIT (if the same)
GREGG'S PIT synonym: Gregg Pear (if the same)
Griffin's Early - see EARLY GRIFFIN

# H

HAMPTON ROUGH synonym: Roughs

HARLEY GUM synonym: Arlingham

HARTPURY GREEN synonyms:Chaceley Green, Chaseley Green, Harpary Green.

HASTINGS

HATHERLEY SQUASH

Hay Pear - see EARLY HAY PEAR and LATE HAY PEAR

Hawfield - see OLDFIELD

Hedgehog Pear - see BARNET

HELLEN'S EARLY synonym: Sweet Huffcap (false)

HELLENS GREEN

HENDRE HUFFCAP synonym: Lumberskull, Yellow Huffcap.

HEYDON

HIGH PEAR synonym:Eye Pear.

HILLEND GREEN synonym: Ford's Green Huffcap, if the same variety.

HOLME LACEY

HOLMER synonyms: Holmore (Knight, by typographical error) Cluster Top, Piddle Pear, Piss Pear, Startlecock, Tun Pear,

Holmore (by typographical error) - see HOLMER

HONEY KNOB synonym: Honeydew

Horse Pear - see GREEN HORSE

Huffcap - see RED HUFFCAP, ROCK and YELLOW HUFFCAP

# I

IRONSIDES

# J

JENKINS RED
JOHN PEAR
JUDGE AMPHLETT
Jug Rumblers - see RUMBLERS

# K

Kings Arms - see YELLOW HUFFCAP
Knap Pear - see KNAPPER
KNAPPER synonym:Napper, Knap Pear.
KNOCK DOWN

# L

Lady Jane - see TUMPER
LATE HAY PEAR synonym: Hay Pear
LATE TAYNTON SQUASH synonym: Taynton Squash
LATE TREACLE synonym: Treacle
Lintot - see NEW MEADOW
Longdon - see GREEN LONGDON, WHITE LONGDON
    and WINNALL'S LONGDON
Longland(s) - see GREEN LONGDON, WHITE
    LONGDON and WINNALL'S LONGDON
Longstalk - see SACK and TURNER'S BARN
Longstuck - see SACK and TURNER'S BARN
LULLAM synonym: Possibly Lulham
LUMBER synonyms: Cumber, Lumber Reds, Pollocks,
    Ram's Cods, Stealyer Balls, Steelyard Balls, Stitter
    Balls, Swaycots.
Lumber Reds - see LUMBER
Lumberskull - see HENDRY HUFFCAP and SOW
    PEAR

# M

Mad Cap - see ROCK
Mad Pear - see ROCK
Malvern Hills - see MOORCROFT
Malvern Pear - see MOORCROFT
MARGARET
MARY PEAR
MERRYLEGS
MICHURIN'S WINTER BEURRE
MILL PEAR
MOORCROFT synonym: Choke Pear, Chokers, Malvern Hill Pear, Malvern Hills, Malvern Pear, Stinking Bishop.
MURRELL

# N

NAILER synonym: Billy Williams
Napper - see KNAPPER
NEWBRIDGE synonym: White Moorcroft
NEW MEADOW synonym: Lintot, Yokehouse
NORMANNISCHEN CIDERBIRNE
Norton Butt - see BUTT

# O

Old Fashioned Longdon - see GREEN LONGDON
Old Squash Pear - see ARLINGHAM SQUASH
Old Taynton Squash - see ARLINGHAM SQUASH
OLDFIELD synonym: Awrel, Hawfield, Offield, Oleville, Ollville.
Ollville - see OLDFIELD

Oleville - see OLDFIELD
Offield - see OLDFIELD

# P

PAINTED LADY
Painted Lady - see BLAKENEY RED
Painted Pear - see BLAKENEY RED
PARSONAGE
PENNY PEAR
PIG PEAR
PINE PEAR
Pine – see PINT
PINT synonym: Pine (in error)
Pixley Red – see RED PEAR
Pollocks - see LUMBER
Port - see WHITE LONGDON
POTATO PEAR

# R

Ram's Cods - see LUMBER
Red Horse - see RED PEAR
RED HUFFCAP synonym: Huffcap, Uffcap, Uffcup.
Red Huffcap - see ROCK
RED LONGDON synonym: Brockhill (false) Brockle,
    Cider Pear, Longland, Red Longland, Red
Red Longley - see RED LONGDON
Red Longney - see RED LONGDON
Red Pear - see BLAKENEY RED
RED PEAR synonym: Aylton Red, Black Horse, Blunt
    Red, Pixley Red, Red Horse, Red Squash Pear, Sack.
Red Squash Pear – see RED PEAR

ROCK synonym: Mad Pear, Mad Cap, Black Huffcap, Brown Huffcap, Red Huffcap, Huffcap, Uffcap, Uffcup.

ROMANIA PERRY PEAR

Rumble Jumble - see RUMBLERS

RUMBLERS synonym: Jug Rumblers, Rumble Jumble.

Roughs - see HAMPTON ROUGH

Russet Longdon - see GREEN LONGDON

# S

SACK synonym: Longstalk, Longstuck. (Probably both in error)

Sack – see RED PEAR

SCHWEIZER WASSERBIRNE

SICKLE PEAR synonym: American Sickle. Possibly: New York Red-cheek, Seckle, Shakespear, Sicker, Lammas of the Americans.

SILVER PEAR synonym: Summer Pear

SNAKE POLE

SOW PEAR synonyms: Pig, Longsnout, Lumberskull, Lomberbrain.

SPEART PEAR synonyms: Spurt pear, Spirit pear, Spirt Pear.

Squash Pear - see ARLINGHAM SQUASH and STAUNTON SQUASH

Squirt Pear – see STAUNTON SQUASH

Startle Cock - see HOLMER

Stanton Squash – see STAUNTON SQUASH

STAUNTON SQUASH synonym: Squash Pear, Squirt Pear, Stanton Squash, White Squash.

Steelyard Balls see LUMBER

Steelyer Balls - see LUMBER

Stinking Bishop - see MOORCROFT
Stitter Balls - see LUMBER
STONY WAY synonym: Stoneyway, Stonyway.
STRAWBERRY PEAR
Summer Pear see SILVER PEAR
Swan see SWAN'S EGG
Swan Egg see SWAN'S EGG
SWAN'S EGG synonyms: Swan, Swan Egg.
Swaycots see LUMBER
SWEET HUFFCAP
Sweet Huffcap - see HELLENS EARLY (false)

# T

Taynton Squash - see EARLY TAYNTON SQUASH
   and LATE TAYNTON SQUASH
TEDDINGTON GREEN synonym: Teddingtons.
Teddingtons - see TEDDINGTON GREEN
THEILERSBIRNE
THORN
THURSTON'S RED synonym: Dymock Red, Billy
   Thurston.
Tom - see TUMPER
Tum - see TUMPER
Tump - see TUMPER
TUMPER synonym: Lady Jane, Tum, Tom, Tumpsee,
   Tump
Tun Pear see HOLMER
TURNER'S BARN synonym: Barn,Longstalk,
   Longstuck.

# U

Uffcap - see RED HUFFCAP, ROCK and YELLOW HUFFCAP

Uffcup - see RED HUFFCAP, ROCK and YELLOW HUFFCAP

# V

VINTAGE FAVOURITE

# W

WATER LUGG

WATFORD

WHITE BACHE synonym: Bache's White, Beech White, White Beech.

White Beech - see WHITE BACHE

White Horse - see WHITE HORSE

WHITE LONGDON synonym: Bastard Barland, Bastard Longdon, Dandoe, Garradine, Longdon, Longland(s), Port,

White Moorcroft - see NEWBRIDGE

White Squash - see STAUNTON SQUASH

WINNALL'S LONGDON synonym: Longdon, Longlands.

# Y

YELLOW HUFFCAP synonym: Black Huffcap , Brown Huffcap, Chandos Huffcap, Green Huffcap, Huffcap, King's Arms, Uffcap, Uffcup, Yellow Longdon, Yellow Longland(s).

Yellow Huffcap - see HENDRE HUFFCAP

Yellow Longdon - see YELLOW HUFFCAP
Yellow Longland(s) - see YELLOW HUFFCAP
Yokehouse - see NEW MEADOW
YOUNG HEYDON

## REFERENCES FOR PERRY PEAR LIST

*Pears of Gloucestershire* by Charles Martell, 2011

*The Apple and Pear as Vintage Fruits.* Robert Hogg, 1886.

*Gloucestershire Perry Pear Varieties* identified by the National Fruit and Cider Institute in 1964.

The best perry pears as listed by Dr. Robert Hogg in his *Fruit Manual* of 1884.

The most important modern varieties of perry pear as designated by the National Fruit and Cider Institute in 1964.

Perry Pears held at the U.S. Department of Agriculture Germplasm Resources Information Network, the USDA Clonal Repository, Corvallis, Oregon.

# SOME HERITAGE FRUIT GROUPS IN AUSTRALIA

**Werribee Park Heritage Orchard,** situated near Melbourne, Australia, is a beautiful antique orchard dating from the 1870s, on the grounds of the old mansion by the Werribee River. It was renowned for its peaches, grapes, apples, quinces, pears, a variety of plums and several other fruits, as well as walnuts and olives. Recently this historic treasure has been rediscovered. Volunteers are replanting and tending the orchard.

www.werribeeparkheritageorchard.org.au

**The Heritage Fruits Society** is also based in Melbourne, Australia. Their aim is to conserve heritage fruit varieties on private and public land. They enable and encourage society members to research this wide range of varieties and to inform the public on the benefits of heritage fruits for health, sustainability and biodiversity.

www.heritagefruitssociety.org.au

**The Heritage and Rare Fruit Network**'s purpose is to provide a forum for sharing information on all varieties of fruit and less common useful plants, to link up people with an interest in growing unusual fruit, and to support sharing of propagation material through grafting days and any other means.

heritageandrarefruits.weebly.com

**The Rare Fruit Society of South Australia** is an amateur organisation of fruit tree growers who preserve heritage varieties, explore climate limita-tions and study propagation, pruning and grafting techniques.

www.rarefruit-sa.org.au

www.ingramcontent.com/pod-product-compliance
Lightning Source LLC
Chambersburg PA
CBHW072210090426
42740CB00012B/2464